Unsat: A Man's Guide To Wedding Etiquette

Unsat: A Man's Guide To Wedding Etiquette

A MODERN GUIDE OF SURVIVAL TECHNIQUES

Kira Wuellner

To order additional copies of this book, contact:
Xlibris Corporation
1-888-795-4274
www.Xlibris.com
Orders@Xlibris.com
97274

Contents

Dedication

Growing up I had two supportive and loving parents who showed me what true love is. Selflessness, care and compassion are three attributes that I have developed throughout my life with my parent's love and guidance and have been longing to share with that special someone. No one has measured up to the love my parents have demonstrated and provided to me, until now. To all the men in the world who are ready to commit to and build this type of love, I wish you good-luck.

Introduction

She walks into the room and your heart stops. Who is this beautiful creature you see? Soon you introduce yourself and the night progresses on from there. Before you know it you are head over heels in love with this woman and are out looking for an engagement ring, to ask her to be your wife. You propose, she accepts and together you chose a date and location for your ceremony and reception. Congratulations, your job is done! You just need to say your vows and kiss your bride. Wrong.

This may not have been the way you met, or the initial feelings that you had for your soon to be wife. Either way you look at it, you are getting married and have a wedding to plan. Weddings are personal. They can be large and extravagant, quick and in a courtroom, small and quaint, or a destination wedding outside of your roots. Weddings are a chance for you and your loved one to reflect your personality through the venue you chose for the ceremony and the reception, as well as the colors and atmosphere that you chose to create.

Once she accepts your proposal, you have just opened Pandora's box of unwritten wedding expectations and etiquette. The title uses the word "unsat", which can be used to describe something that is unsatisfactory or not acceptable. Many of you are unaware of this term, and will probably make it part of your vocabulary after learning what their responsibilities are now that you have popped the question. This book is designed to give you the inside scoop from a bride's perspective on her unspoken expectations for you. Use this book as a way to read what quite possibly is going on in your bride's mind, and to be her supportive knight in shining armor before, during and after your wedding day.

Chapter 1

BEFORE THE WEDDING DAY

Before you get married there is a lot of behind the scenes planning and preparing. Here are suggestions for steps to complete to ensure a happily ever after wedding day.

Ask permission

Asking permission to take someone's daughters hand in marriage is crucial to continuing harmony through both families, especially the parents of your bride to be. By asking permission from the bride's parents, especially her father, you are showing respect to the family and asking permission to take over the initial care and well being of their daughter. This can be done over the phone, through a letter, or most commonly face to face. Some cultures may just ask for the blessing and permission of the family, while other cultures exchange cattle and other livestock when asking permission as presenting a gift in exchange. When asking permission for marriage, it is usually a conversation that is kept between you and who you have asked. If you're wife to be were to find out that you have asked permission for her hand in marriage, most likely she will know that your proposal is coming, which could ruin any opportunity for surprise screams, hysterical crying and a lot of jumping around.

Notes

Rings

When it comes to deciding on an engagement ring, the decision most likely falls on the shoulders of the bride. Some men propose with a ring that the bride has already picked out, or else she might not accept a proposal. Some couples will go ring shopping together and narrow it down to a few select rings that would equally make the bride happy, and the man light headed. Other couples will talk about getting engaged and spending the rest of their lives together and the man will go out and pick out the engagement ring without his better half. To each their own. Chances are that your soon bride-to-be fits into one of these categories.

The timeless argument that continues to come up time and time again, is does size matter? Now guys, I am not talking about your twig and berries, but the size and total weight of the diamond on the ring. Some couples decided on a different stone because it may be more memorable or the bride-to-be may not care for diamonds, but majority of men buy diamond engagement rings. The center cut diamond, which is the biggest is where the size is determined.

Will this center stone be one carat, ¾ carat, ½ carat, or pump it up to 1½ carats or even more? That is your decision, since chances are this ring is coming out of your paycheck. Some women have small fingers and a large ring might look awkward, while other ladies will take what they are given. The total weight of the ring is the weight of the center stone in combination with any side or accent diamonds the ring may This is the ring that she will wear for the rest of her life, everyday, which symbolizes the love and commitment that the two of you share. Just a thought.

The wedding band sometimes will come in a set with the engagement ring, but often times couples will go shopping between the engagement and before the wedding to buy wedding bands together. Some couples feel comfortable having matching or complementary wedding bands. Other couples chose to have it made of the same material or pick it out together. While some couples each pick out their wedding band, which complements the engagement ring setting and fits the style and personality of the individual. This is a decision that can be made together after the engagement, but yes guys; there is another ring to seal the deal.

Notes

_____

_____

_____

_____

_____

_____

_____

_____

_____

_____

_____

_____

_____

_____

_____

_____

_____

_____

Setting the scene

Congratulations! If you are reading this part of the book she has accepted your proposal and has not left you in the dust with a non-returnable ring and broke. Now that people will stop asking you when you are going to propose you can move on and make the choice together on where you want your wedding ceremony to be and where the party will take place, because you have a lot to celebrate (and plan)! The first question to decide on is where the ceremony will take place and what you would like the atmosphere to feel like. Couples get married in churches, synagogues, parks, and restaurants, in a back yard, on a boat, on a tropical island and even in another country. As a couple it is your decision where to have the ceremony and get hitched! Your religion and its guidelines may guide this, or your free spirit may send you away. Since this is your wedding, ultimately it is your choice.

After you have chosen where to hold your ceremony, the next step is to set the venue to host your wedding reception. If getting married in a house of religion, you will most likely rent out a venue to host your wedding reception. If getting married outside of a house of religion your wedding ceremony may also host your wedding reception. Many resorts and destination weddings host the ceremony and reception at the same place, just located in different areas. This is also important because you are given the choice of celebrating indoors or outdoors or a mixture of both. Many venues offer an area for dinner and a reception, which will also provide access to the outdoors such as a balcony or patio. This is a wonderful option when keeping the weather in mind (no, we cannot control it) as well as guests who may smoke or want a celebratory cigar smoke, in a building with smoking restrictions.

Notes

_____

_____

_____

_____

_____

_____

_____

_____

_____

_____

_____

_____

_____

_____

_____

_____

_____

_____

Los Colores

We're not in Mexico anymore, but perhaps that is one of your choices for a destination wedding. Regardless, the next step in planning a wedding is picking out the colors for your wedding. Many couples may pick one main color, green, and have an accent color of blue. The reason it is so important for your fiancé (yes, she now has a title and is no longer your girlfriend) to decide on a color is because it will be reflected in the rest of your wedding. The bridesmaid's dresses will reflect the color; your décor at the ceremony and reception will display the color as will your cake, drinks and flowers. If you are a man who honestly does not care, tell her that it doesn't matter to you and that what she picks will make you happy. Do not, I repeat, do not say "whatever", "I don't care", "It doesn't matter" or anything along these lines. Give a hoot or close your beak. This will make her happy to know where you stand on the color so she can book a floral appointment and start looking for bridesmaid dresses. Take a deep breath, most brides-to-be will not need or ask for your assistance at the floral appointment or shopping with her bridesmaids. If you are one of the unlucky few, good luck to you and have a brew or two.

Notes

_____

_____

_____

_____

_____

_____

_____

_____

_____

_____

_____

_____

_____

_____

_____

_____

_____

_____

Attire

To tux or not to tux, that is the question. Most likely your wedding party (men) will wear a tux if your wedding is of black tie status, or quite formal. The competitor to the tux is a suit. Both are fancy, but one may have a bow tie and stripe down the pant leg, while the other one may be worn again if bought, and is a little less formal. Either way both can be rented. If your choice is a destination wedding, I am not sure of many men who would like to get married on the beach in a tuxedo when it is 95 degrees out and sunny without a breeze. Many times the atmosphere of the wedding along with the theme will decide between a tux or a suit, a suit or a collared shirt, khaki's and flip flops.

The one unwritten rule that I am now writing down is regardless of attire, the groom does not pay for it. Simon says that if you are having a wedding and getting married, the chances of you standing up as an attendant in a buddy's wedding is coming your way or has already passed you and you have paid for your attire—usually a daily rental fee. Bridesmaids usually spend hundreds of dollars on a dress they will only wear once, groomsmen usually spend a hundred dollars on a suit or tux they will only wear once. You have the easy side of the deal, just go with it and pay your way when you are in other's weddings, but do not pay for your groomsmen's rental fees, it will come back to bite you in the end.

Notes

_____

_____

_____

_____

_____

_____

_____

_____

_____

_____

_____

_____

_____

_____

_____

_____

_____

_____

Invitations

Deciding who will come to your wedding can be quite easy or challenging. Begin by making a list of important people to you (not your parents) that you want to be at your special day. Have your fiancé make a list of hers as well. Then bring your lists together to make a solid list of individuals that you both would like to attend. Depending on how many people you want to be at your wedding you can then bring the lists to your parents and see if there are any important people you are missing, or anyone they would like to attend that are close family friends. Many times the venue where your reception will be held will have a maximum for capacity so you can have a rough idea of what numbers to stay around. When you do finalize your list of guests invited to your wedding, remember to include anyone who will be accompanying the guest or providing the opportunity to bring a date. These choices will impact your initial count of what to expect as far as attendance at your big day.

Choosing the invitations to your wedding is usually something couples do together, some even chose to make and print their own if they have the means to. If you chose to send out "save the date" cards, this should be done four to six months before the wedding date. There are many fun ways to do this from refrigerator magnets, to holiday greeting cards. Save the date cards allow your guests, especially any that will be traveling to make proper accommodations and changes to their schedules as needed ahead of time so they can attend your big day!

The invitations to your wedding should be mailed out eight weeks before your wedding date. This allows time for individuals to make plans and make a commitment to your big day. The RSVP day on your invitations should be planned to be about three weeks prior to your wedding. This allows for last minute adjustments on dinner, place cards, as well as party favors and guest cards. Included in your invitation should be the address, name and directions to the ceremony site and to the reception. Many people have GPS now days, but written instructions can be useful, especially to guests who might not be familiar with your ceremony and reception locations.

As stuffed as the envelope may be, also include recommended accommodations where your guests can spend the night if they have a significant travel distance, are from out of town, or just want to party until they drop! Usually suggest two hotels and include their telephone number as well as the address. If you call ahead and notify the hotel that you are having your wedding in town, most likely you will be able to hold a group of hotel rooms, at a reduced rate. It is important to put this information on the accommodations sheet, so guests know to mention your wedding, to receive the discounted rate.

Once your guests have booked rooms at a hotel, find out where they are staying. Knowing how many people are traveling in from out of town to spend the night will make this next step much easier and smoother. Providing a gift basket or bag of goodies for your guests who have traveled and are staying over night is a great way to say "thanks for eating our free food and drinking our free beer, but you have to pay for the hotel room". These gift bags can be themed towards that of your wedding or even provide hangover relief in the morning. Items such as bottled water, granola bars, gum, fresh fruit, lotion, condoms and candy are always quick and easy favorites. Once the gift bags are ready, they can be dropped off at the hotel and put behind the desk, the night before the wedding. Most hotels are more than welcoming to give the gift bags to the guests as they check in their reservation, under the wedding party block of names. Just remember to label the gift bags especially if some are reserved for your grandparents, and others given to your friends may be a bit taboo for family to receive.

Notes

Feast like a king!

Food. The way to a man's heart is through food. Did your fiancé ever cook for you or bake for you. That's because she knew the way to your heart, and now you have bought her the diamond ring she has dreamed of. The three main points of the wedding day are the food, drinks, and cake! It is your wedding so you can use your preferences when hiring a caterer or having to choose from a prepared menu. However, if you are my sister, you can also have taco bell catered in. It's your day so let your delicacies reflect your love and let the feast begin!

Most venues' and caterer's allow for their options of food to be tasted so you and your bride can decide on which dishes to serve. Some couples do a buffet style wedding where the guests can serve themselves, while others have meals prepared and served to the guests once seated. Usually a vegetarian dish is one of the selections to provide an option for all guests. There are usually two other meats that are chosen, such as chicken and beef, or fish and chicken. Either way, the decision will be made by your taste buds! Make sure you arrive on an empty stomach so you can enjoy all the varieties of foods that are at your fingertips to be tasted.

Now that you have eaten your thirst must be quenched! There are many options for you to provide at your reception for your guests to drink. You can choose from tap beer, pitchers of beer, kegs and barrels of beer, as well as domestic and international imports depending on your taste and that of your guests. Wine there is always the choice or red or white, as well as the quality. Once again, this is up to you and your fiancé. The choice for liquor at your reception is also guided by your preference. Some venues have packages that might include beer and wine but not liquor, or a type of a different combination.

To put a new twist on your reception and to make it more personal, you also have the option of making a signature drink to match the theme or mood of your reception. Most bartenders will have about three ideas premade for you to decide from that can be served during your cocktail hour. These drinks are usually fun, fruity and inviting to your guests. So now that you have filled your belly on food tasting, you get to wash it down with tasting the signature drinks that you can chose from and offer during your cocktail hour.

Now that you've had your food and drink its time for dessert! Most commonly couples attend a cake tasting together at a bakery or specialty shop they have chosen. At the tasting you literally get to sit and eat cake! You have the ability to try all the flavors you can imagine; have your cake and eat it too! Once you have narrowed down the flavors you like you get to pick out the design of your cake. If you are looking to be more out of the box you can consider using cupcakes instead of cake, or using a candy station. Candy stations are set up at a table with little gift bags or boxes and have container, usually clear glass, filled with candy that compliments your favorites, the colors of the wedding, or the mood of the wedding. These can be used in addition to a cake or cupcakes, as a to-go option for guests that stay late at the reception or a replacement for a cake.

Notes

_____

_____

_____

_____

_____

_____

_____

_____

_____

_____

_____

_____

_____

_____

_____

_____

_____

_____

_____

Rehearsal Dinner

The night before your wedding day, you will have a rehearsal at the church, which is followed by a rehearsal dinner. At the church rehearsal you will be able to practice what your job will be on the next day, besides kissing your bride. This can be sometimes long and tiresome, but keep positive and remind yourself that beer is only a short time away. After the rehearsal is completed at the location of your ceremony, usually the wedding party, readers, ushers and their guests, as well as guests that may be traveling from out of town are invited to your rehearsal dinner. It can be formal or informal; outside or inside, self serve or plate service. It is a time to celebrate the coming together of two families and to thank everyone in your wedding party while you have the chance because tomorrow will be a busy day!

Commonly at the rehearsal dinner, the bride gives her bridesmaids a gift, thanking them for standing up in her wedding and bearing witness to her marriage. The groomsmen are also given gifts for the same reason. It is up to you and your fiancé what to get the attendants in your wedding. Many times couples will give a token of appreciation to both parents as well as anyone who may be doing a reading in church or ushering during the service. The one unspoken, usually undisputed rule of the rehearsal dinner is the groom's parent's pay for it, while the bride's family pays for the wedding day festivities and reception.

Notes

_____

_____

_____

_____

_____

_____

_____

_____

_____

_____

_____

_____

_____

_____

_____

_____

_____

_____

_____

_____

_____

Tips

When you go out to the bars you tip your bartender. When you eat at a restaurant you tip your server. When valet parking a vehicle you tip your driver, and when your fiancé goes to get her hair and nails done, she tips her stylist and nail technician. So, with that being pounded into your brain, this next "tip" should be quite simple. Before your wedding day be sure you have set aside in labeled envelopes with the name of your vendor, florist, D.J., and any other part of the entertainment with their tip included. I am not going to tell you how much to tip these businesses, but this is their business and life as well.

Tomorrow is your wedding day. Kiss your fiancé for the last time, as your next kiss will be as husband and wife. Have some drinks tonight to celebrate and hang out with your buddies doing guy things tonight. Plan on not seeing your bride until tomorrow morning as she walks down the isle. My tip to you is to get a good night sleep because tomorrow is going to be a day full of fun and celebrating! Waking up to a hangover is not the way your bride will want to meet you at the end of the isle . . . save that for Sunday morning.

Notes

_____

_____

_____

_____

_____

_____

_____

_____

_____

_____

_____

_____

_____

_____

_____

_____

_____

_____

_____

Chapter 2

THE WEDDING DAY

You have just spent months if not over a year preparing for this day, the day she will become your wife and you will kiss your bride! There are minimal responsibilities for you on this day besides celebrating and having a blast! Many small things can be taken care of by a friend or your parents. Here are some suggestions for a smooth wedding day, guaranteed not to be a buzz kill.

A *gift to be simple*

You are probably thinking, "a gift? I just bought her a diamond engagement and wedding band!" I agree, I would be thinking the same thing! The tradition behind exchanging gifts on the morning of your wedding is following the practice of you do not spend the night together before your wedding day. These gifts are to reflect your feelings for her, and to ensure her that you will be waiting at the end of the isle for her. If its any consequence, she will be most likely buying you a grooms gift as well. Some couples discuss this ahead of time, while others may mention or pick up on a special gift they want to exchange on their wedding day. On the other hand, some couples decide not to do it; I just caution that if you are not going to do it you make that well known, so she is not giving you a gift and you are empty handed and feeling like an ass.

These gifts can be handmade or bought. Since this book has nothing to do with a bride reading it, I'm going to let you in on another little secret. For your gift to your bride, start with a greeting card and a personally written message in it from you. If you chose to give her a gift, there is a saying that on a bride's wedding day she has to wear something bought & blue, something old & something new. You could buy her something new or give her something blue. Majority of men chose to buy a piece of jewelry that she can wear on her wedding day, such as earrings she really wants, a bracelet or necklace. It could also be jewelry made of a blue stone to be her something blue.

Other ideas that can be considered for your bride on the morning of your wedding is something that is personalize or engraved that she can use, or something that is meaningful between the two of you. There are many ideas if you go to a jeweler, they can clearly help you. Also asking friends and researching bride's gift on the Internet can bring up new ideas for you as well as opportunities to personalize and engrave things. Give the gift to the bride's mother or maid of honor, someone she will be with the morning of your wedding, so she can give it to your bride. The purpose and goal of the bride's gift on the morning of your wedding is to reassure her that she is the one you want to marry and that you are just as in love with her, as she is with you.

Notes

_____

_____

_____

_____

_____

_____

_____

_____

_____

_____

_____

_____

_____

_____

_____

_____

_____

_____

_____

Photos

Photography of a wedding is a very personal aspect. Some couples hire a photographer, which they chose, some chose friends with a photography business, while other will have a family member photograph their wedding. The one thing to remember when choosing a photographer is that these photos cannot be relived and acted out again. They serve as memories of your wedding day. It is important to find a photographer that you and your fiancé feel comfortable with and their style compliments yours.

Guys usually do not like getting their photos taken, so to ease up part of the pain, it would be a good idea if you have your photographer take group photos of you and your groomsmen before the wedding and the bride and her bridesmaid, that way only a few pictures have to be taken in church. You can even have individual pictures with parents and family members before the ceremony as well to decrease the time after the ceremony, so you can get your drink and party on!

Adding a slideshow to your reception usually gets a standing ovation. Starting the show off with pictures of you and your wife growing up, and then pictures of the two of you during the development of your relationship and you "wooing" her. These slide shows allow guests of the bride and yourself to get to know a little of the past that you had prior to your wedding and the life of your bride, as well as making them feel a part of your relationship and important to you, especially by including photos with friends and family members.

Notes

Tip out

You have your envelopes already stuffed with the checks for your vendors and labeled to whom it belongs. All that needs to be completed is to pass out the tips to the vendors. You can choose to give out your tips together as a married couple to thank the vendor for their services, or you can assign it to a family member to decrease your responsibility on your big day!

Notes

_____

_____

_____

_____

_____

_____

_____

_____

_____

_____

_____

_____

_____

_____

_____

_____

_____

_____

_____

To *see or not to see?*

The choice to see your bride on the day of your wedding before she walks down the isle is up to you and her. There is a superstition that it brings bad luck, but it is between the two of you to decide if you want to see each other before you walk down the isle on your wedding day or not. Many girls dream of walking down the isle in a beautiful dress and dream of the feeling they will get when she lock eyes with her soon to be husband. Other men and women may faint at the thought of this and would prefer a private meeting and taking photos together before the ceremony. Regardless of your choice, it is yours and only yours to make with your fiancé. It is your big day; make it happen your way.

Notes

_____

_____

_____

_____

_____

_____

_____

_____

_____

_____

_____

_____

_____

_____

_____

_____

_____

_____

_____

_____

_____

Toast

White or wheat? Butter or jelly? Just kidding, I am not talking about a side of toast to go with your bacon and eggs, but instead your chance to let everyone at your reception know, how you feel about your new bride. The first goal of your day should be to keep sober enough to annunciate your toast and to make your bride feel special in front of all your guests. Some guys write their toast ahead of time, while others pull it together on the spot. Either way, don't have your guests leaving your reception remembering your toast as a drunken spectacle.

Your toast can be whatever you like to make it, but including something along the lines of why you are so happy to be marrying your wife is always nice. Your bride will give a toast, the fathers usually do, as well as the best man and maid of honor. Most toasts take place at the beginning of dinner and provide entertainment for your guests as they wait for their food to arrive. I highly emphasize keeping out the cuss words, and attempting to make your audience laugh. Note to self: toast with butter and jelly will help your hangover the morning after.

Notes

_____

_____

_____

_____

_____

_____

_____

_____

_____

_____

_____

_____

_____

_____

_____

_____

_____

_____

_____

_____

Keep it on

After the meal has been served its time to get your full drink on! I have a rule for the man I marry: stay sober enough until 10:00 p.m. and then get as wasted as you want, just don't throw up on my thousand dollar wedding dress! The reason I suggest 10:00 p. m. is because most guests who are just being social and not using you for your free alcohol will leave usually no later than 10:00 p.m. It is important for you as the host to be coherent enough to say "thank you for coming" and "good bye". After then the night is all yours. This does not mean you cannon start drinking when you wake up, as most brides do to calm their nerves, just pace yourself throughout your day.

Be sure to keep your wedding attire suit/tux on throughout the entire night, especially if it is a rental. If you misplace any parts of the rental it will be your responsibility to pay for it and most rentals are due back the following morning. By all means, feel free to take off your suit or tux coat, but leave rest of the garb on. Some dancing machines chose to take off their shoes, which most bridesmaids and bride's will do so that gives you the unwritten rule that it is fair game for you to do it as well. Dance, drink, and be merry and make sure you can still get it up to consummate the marriage and make it official!

Notes

_____

_____

_____

_____

_____

_____

_____

_____

_____

_____

_____

_____

_____

_____

_____

_____

_____

_____

_____

_____

Chapter 3

AFTER THE WEDDING DAY

The morning after your wedding day is still full of guests, surprises and hangovers. Here are a few ideas to make the days following your wedding less of a headache.

Hangover breakfast

The morning after your wedding night is started off with a hangover breakfast and gift opening. A nice idea for this is a brunch that can be at someone's home; catered in to a venue or held at a restaurant that provides buffet style brunch. Customary, it is the financial responsibility of the groom's parents to pay for the gift opening meal in addition to the rehearsal dinner. This meal has great healing power for any hangovers that might be looming in the air; also included should be water and Bloody Mary's. At the breakfast, as people are eating, it is also customary to open the gifts that you and your bride received for your wedding day. Make sure that someone, usually one of your parents, are writing down what you got as you open the gift and who it was from. This makes the next step 100% easier.

Notes

Thank you cards

A small token to show your appreciation, other than the meal and alcohol you provided, is to send a thank you card to the guests who attended your wedding day. It is customary to send thank you cards, especially to guest who gave you a gift, and to personally take the time to thank them for the gift they gave you. If you look back at your list that was written down from the gift opening, it should make this part a breeze.

One way to make this step even easier is to take a favorite photo of the two of you and make photo thank you cards! These can be sent to everyone who gave gifts along with everyone who registered in your gift book. They can include a simple message of thanks and gratitude for your guests who took time out of their busy schedule to share your special day with you. The photo thank you cards are much easier, because all you have to do is address and stamp the envelope. Now go back to your room and make boom-boom with your new bride!

Congratulations you did it! You survived the preparation before your wedding, your wedding day, and the morning after. Good luck to you on the rest of your lives together and may the future bring you more happiness and joy than the days leading up to your wedding.

Notes

www.ingramcontent.com/pod-product-compliance
Lightning Source LLC
Chambersburg PA
CBHW050338290526
45785CB00006B/2548